HUMAN BODY BASICS

Did you know that you have something in common with every single living thing – from palm trees to parrots, snakes to sea lions? You and they are known as 'organisms' – a group that includes all living things. As organisms, we all do seven key things: breathe, feed, excrete, grow, move, feel and reproduce. These are the seven 'life processes'.

epithelial cells

Lots of epithelial cells join together to make tissue. This tissue forms the thin linings, or membranes, within the lungs.

Smallest parts

Each and every organism is made of cells – trillions of them! Cells are the smallest building blocks of every living thing. They are so small that they cannot be seen without a microscope. All cells have the same basic parts, but they vary depending on the job that they do.

Your lungs are the main organs in your respiratory system. They are made of many different types of cells and tissue.

Tissue and organs

Tissue is formed by lots of the same type of cell joining together in sheets. Different tissues connect together to form organs.

Body systems

Your body's organs work together in systems. Your body systems take care of different life processes.

The lungs work with other organs in your respiratory system to allow you to take air in and push it out of your body.

YOUR BREATHTAKING LUNGS

You breathe in about 15 times every minute, more if you are exercising. The air you breathe travels through roughly 2,000km of airways – passages that take air deep into your lungs. It's an impressive set-up… but what is it for?

Why do I breathe?

You breathe to get air into and out of microscopic air sacs within your lungs. From the outside, a healthy lung looks pink and spongy. You have two lungs, one on each side of your chest. They are surrounded by rows of bones, called ribs. These form a protective barrier called your ribcage.

Air contains a mixture of gases. About 20% of air is a gas called oxygen. You need a constant supply of oxygen to stay alive. Your brain, liver, heart and other organs and muscles, for example, all need oxygen. You can survive days without water, and weeks without food – but you would last only a few minutes without oxygen.

The higher up you climb, the less oxygen there is in the air. Many mountain climbers carry breathing equipment containing oxygen.

YOUR BREATHTAKING LUNGS

and ← ROCKING

respiratory system

FIND OUT HOW YOUR BODY WORKS!

Paul Mason

CONTENTS

When the air you breathe in reaches your lungs, the oxygen is removed and absorbed into your blood, ready to be distributed around the rest of your body. The oxygen is used to release energy from the food you eat. This energy is needed by every part of your body to keep it working.

You need to breathe for another reason, too. Getting energy from food creates a waste gas called carbon dioxide. Breathing out gets rid of this gas.

nostril

mouth

windpipe

lung

lung

diaphragm

DON'T TRY THIS AT HOME!

Most people can go without breathing for between 20 and 45 seconds. After specialist training, though, some people can hold their breath for MUCH longer than that. In 2012, freediver Stig Severinsen set a world record by holding his breath underwater for TWENTY-TWO MINUTES!

Holding your breath for a long time without training is dangerous, so really DON'T try this at home.

Freedivers dive down to great depths without the use of a breathing apparatus.

STRANGE BUT TRUE!

Babies start life taking 40–50 breaths per minute. By the time they are five or six years old, though, the number of breaths they take per minute has shrunk to about 15. That's the same as an adult.

NOSTRILS AND MOUTH

Your nose and mouth are the starting point for your respiratory system, where air is drawn in. They are also the security guards – part of their job is to stop anything getting in that shouldn't be there.

Keeping out intruders

You need a constant supply of air reaching your lungs to keep you alive. You don't really want anything else getting into your lungs, though. It could damage the airways, or the lungs themselves. So it's a good job your body is able to keep out any unwelcome guests.

The hairy bogey trap

One way unwelcome guests could get into your respiratory system is through your nostrils. Fortunately, these have some very effective defences.

Hairs in your nostrils trap dirt and germs – two of the three main ingredients of bogeys. (The other one is mucus, sticky stuff from further up your nostrils.) This is a good reason not to eat your bogeys – they could contain microbes.

Further inside the nasal passages are microscopic hairs called cilia. These are coated with sticky mucus, which traps any leftover dirt and microbes. The cilia are constantly moving to and fro. As they do this, they move the mucus, dirt and germs out of your nasal passages.

Tiny hair-like cells called cilia are your nose's clean-up crew.

Pieces of food

You use your mouth not only for breathing, but also for eating. But getting food in your lungs would be a really bad idea! To stop this happening, you have an epiglottis. The epiglottis is a leaf-shaped flap of skin that changes its position, depending on whether you are breathing or swallowing. Normally, the epiglottis is open, which allows you to breathe. When you swallow some food or drink, though, the flap closes and stops food getting into your lungs.

See for yourself

You know that your nose helps you smell things - but did you know it's also important for TASTE? This is because the taste of your food is actually made up of about 80% smell.

To test this for yourself, hold your nose next time you eat something. Does it taste as strong as usual, without smell making a contribution?

LOOK CLOSER
EPIGLOTTIS

The epiglottis is open for breathing.

The epiglottis closes when you swallow.

air

epiglottis

mouth

mouth

food pipe

epiglottis

windpipe

food pipe

windpipe

DID YOU KNOW?

Horses can't breathe through their mouths.

Horses can only breathe through their nostrils. A flap of tissue forms a tight seal at the back of the mouth, sealing it off from the throat. The flap only opens when the horse wants to swallow food or water.

JOURNEY TO THE LUNGS

BRILLIANT BODY FACT

In your lifetime, you'll breathe at least 250 million litres of air!

At first, the air you breathe and the food you eat share an entry passage into your body – the throat, or pharynx. Soon, though, the air enters its own tube, the trachea. This leads to a maze of passageways that take air into the lungs.

Trachea and bronchi

After you breathe it in, air goes past the epiglottis (see page 7) and is pulled into the trachea, which is also known as the 'windpipe'. Like parts of your nose, the trachea is lined with cilia. These tiny hairs trap and expel dirt and germs.

Next, the trachea divides into two bronchi, taking air towards either your left or right lung. The bronchi sub-divide, so that they can deliver air to different parts of your lungs. You might think that's it – the air has passed along the bronchi and is in your lungs – great! But the air isn't at the end of its journey yet.

LOOK CLOSER
INSIDE THE LUNGS

throat or pharynx

epiglottis

food tube leading to stomach

trachea

bronchi

bronchioles

lung

diaphragm

lung

The airways inside the lungs branch into smaller and smaller tubes.

The bronchioles

The bronchi feed air into smaller tubes called bronchioles. The bronchioles split again and again, so that the whole of your lung is lined with a network of tiny air passages. The smallest are only as thick as cotton thread. They are so tiny that there's room for about 30,000 of them in EACH LUNG!

STRANGE BUT TRUE!

Most adults can hold a maximum of about 5 litres of air in their lungs — but there are exceptions. The Spanish cyclist Miguel Indurain, for example, had amazingly large, 8-litre lungs. Indurain's lungs were SO big that they pushed his stomach down and outward — giving Indurain a little pot belly, even though he was super fit!

See for yourself

Find out how much air your lungs hold!

Take a large, empty drinks bottle and fill it with water. Half fill a washing up bowl with water. Cover the end of the bottle, so that no water spills out, then turn the bottle upside down in the washing up bowl, and uncover the end.

Take a bendy straw and put the short section into the opening of the bottle under the water. Let the longer end stick up out of the water.

Take a deep breath, and blow into the long end of the straw for as long as you can.

The amount of air in the bottle is the amount that was in your lungs.

DID YOU KNOW?

Your lungs are different sizes.

Not only are your lungs slightly different sizes, they also have different structures. The right lung is bigger and has three lobes. The left lung is smaller and has only two lobes.

The difference is because your heart tilts to the left, so it takes up more space on the left side of your chest.

right lung

left lung

upper lobe

upper lobe

middle lobe

lower lobe

lower lobe

heart

THE ALVEOLUS

OXYGEN EXCHANGE

The lungs are your only organs that would float, if removed. They can do this because they contain millions of miniature air sacs, called alveoli. Each alveolus (the name for just one of the air sacs) contains only a tiny amount of air – but you have a LOT of them. Together they hold enough air to keep the lungs afloat.

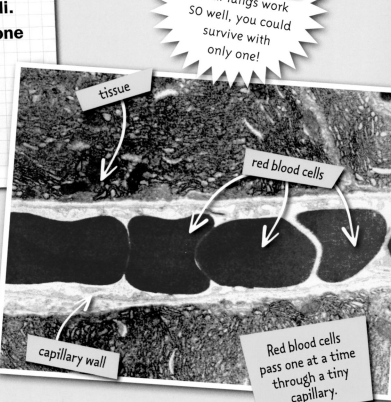

tissue

red blood cells

capillary wall

Red blood cells pass one at a time through a tiny capillary.

Amazing alveoli

At the end of the tiniest bronchioles in each lung are the alveoli. You have about 600 million alveoli altogether! That's so many in total that if they were all spread out flat on the ground, you could easily cover a tennis court with them.

Wrapped around each alveolus are tiny blood vessels called capillaries. These are SO tiny that blood cells have to pass through them one at a time. Between the alveolus and the capillary is a membrane just one cell thick. This is so thin that FIFTY of them on top of one another would only be as thick as tissue paper.

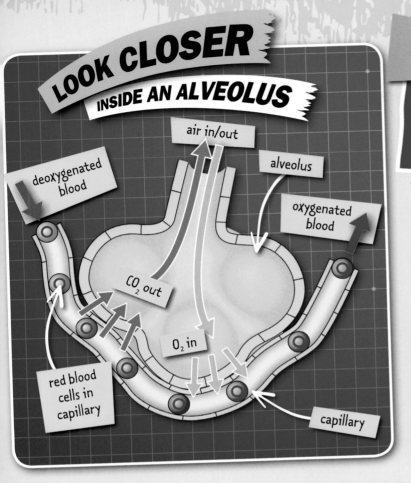

air in/out

deoxygenated blood

alveolus

oxygenated blood

CO_2 out

O_2 in

red blood cells in capillary

capillary

STRANGE BUT TRUE!

The word 'lung' probably comes from an Old English word, 'lunge'. This meant 'light' — as in, not weighing very much.

Exchanging gases

The alveolus's job is to deliver oxygen (O_2) to your blood. As you breathe in, the alveolus fills with air containing oxygen. As the blood moves along the capillaries, oxygen passes through the thin membrane, from the alveolus into the capillary. At the same time, a waste gas called carbon dioxide (CO_2) passes into the alveolus ready to be breathed out.

DON'T TRY THIS AT HOME!

In the early 1500s, doctors thought sickness was caused by having too much of one of the four 'humours'. A German doctor called Paracelsus had other ideas.

Paracelsus noticed that miners often had sicknesses of their lungs — so he got hold of some dead miners, and cut them open to see what was wrong. It turned out that dust from the mines, not excessive humours, was causing the miners' sickness.

DID YOU KNOW?

Your blood can carry a LOT of oxygen.

Red blood cells contain a substance called hemoglobin. It's hemoglobin that carries oxygen around the body.

Each hemoglobin molecule can carry four oxygen molecules — and a SINGLE red blood cell contains about 250 million hemoglobin molecules. So in theory there could be a billion oxygen molecules on a single red blood cell!

OXYGEN DELIVERY, WASTE COLLECTION

As oxygen has been collected from the alveoli, it leaves your respiratory system and enters your circulatory system. From here it goes on a journey around the body, first to the heart and then on to where it is most needed.

Delivering and collecting

When the oxygen-rich blood leaves your lungs, it heads straight for your heart. From there, the blood is pumped out to the rest of your body through your circulatory system. Blood is first pumped into arteries that carry the oxygen-rich blood to the cells of your body.

When blood reaches a place in your body that needs oxygen, the tissue pulls the oxygen out of the blood through the thin capillary walls. The tissue might be part of a muscle, your brain, your liver or kidneys, your eyes, almost anywhere! As the oxygen is used, waste products are created. Among these is a gas called carbon dioxide.

LOOK CLOSER
CIRCULATORY SYSTEM

Arteries are shown in red, veins are shown in blue.

head and arms

lung

lung

liver

heart

stomach

kidneys

legs and body

tissue cells

Carbon dioxide moves out of tissue cells and into red blood cells and blood plasma.

red blood cell

Oxygen moves out of the red blood cells and blood plasma into tissue cells.

Dangerous waste

Too much carbon dioxide is poisonous to humans, so your body needs to get rid of the excess as soon as possible! Your blood collects the carbon dioxide (there's room aboard, now that the oxygen has been delivered) and returns to the heart through your veins. The blood carries the carbon dioxide to your heart, which pumps it to your lungs. There, it rejoins the respiratory system: the carbon dioxide passes into the alveoli and is breathed out.

STRANGE BUT TRUE!

Many people breathe mainly through one nostril at a time. Their body changes nostrils regularly, and the change can happen after a few minutes or several hours. It has been claimed that which nostril you are mainly using has important effects. The right nostril is claimed to increase the level of glucose energy in your blood, and to draw in more oxygen than the left nostril.

DID YOU KNOW?

How freedivers breathe

You breathe to feed your body's need for oxygen, and to get rid of carbon dioxide.

Freedivers use special breathing techniques to lower the amount of carbon dioxide in their blood. This is what makes it possible for them to hold their breath for an amazingly long time.

BREATH CONTROL

You don't always breathe the same amount. Chasing your friend on a bicycle, for example, makes you breathe faster and deeper than walking very slowly to a maths lesson. So how does your body know when, and how much, to breathe?

The brilliant brain stem

Your breathing is controlled by an area at the base of your brain called the brain stem. Your nervous system is constantly feeding it information about your blood vessels, muscles and lungs. The brain stem uses this information to work out whether changes to your breathing are needed.

When you ride a bike fast, your muscles need extra energy. So that they get it, the brain stem sends a signal saying, 'breathe faster'. More breaths mean more oxygen reaching your lungs and blood. Your body uses this oxygen to provide your muscles with extra energy.

Exercise uses oxygen to burn fuel in your body for energy. A waste product is carbon dioxide, which is released into the blood. Your body needs to get rid of any excess carbon dioxide, since this can be poisonous.

brain stem

1. The body records high levels of carbon dioxide in the blood.

2. The brain stem receives messages from the body.

3. The lungs are instructed to breathe harder.

4. Carbon dioxide is expelled and more oxygen is taken in.

Later, when you are walking to maths, your muscles need less energy than when you were racing on your bike. The brain stem tells your lungs it's OK to breathe more slowly.

Emotional breathing

Next time you watch a scary movie, stop and notice whether your breathing changes. It probably will! Your emotions affect your breathing. Feeling afraid or excited makes people breathe harder.

Experts think this is an old instinct from our early human ancestors. They would feel afraid when they saw something dangerous – a wolf or bear, perhaps. Their brain stems arranged an early delivery of oxygen, ready for running away or fighting.

BREATHING— NOT THAT SIMPLE!

BRILLIANT BODY FACT

Your lungs contain 'stretch receptors' to stop them expanding too much!

How do you breathe? You probably won't be able to answer that question without reading the rest of this page. That's because we all breathe automatically. This makes breathing seem simple – so it might surprise you to find out that it is actually quite complicated.

Breathing in air

Taking a breath starts with your diaphragm, a dome-shaped layer of muscle below your lungs. When you need to breathe in, your diaphragm shrinks downwards and flattens out. This pulls the bottom of your lungs downwards too. They expand and pull in air.

More muscles

The muscles between your ribs also help you breathe. They tighten and pull your ribcage upwards and outwards. This helps your lungs expand and draw in air. Finally, muscles in your belly, and in your neck and shoulders, also swing into action when you take a breath. And all this happens between 15 and 60 times a minute!

LOOK CLOSER
BREATHING IN

Air is pulled into the lungs.

The lungs expand.

The diaphragm stretches flat and downwards.

Your lungs are roughly cone shaped. The wide base is attached to your diaphragm.

Slippery lungs

To be able to pull in air, your lungs have to be able to expand and deflate inside your chest. But how do they do this without rubbing against your ribcage? It's thanks to the pleura, a double membrane that surrounds each lung. One membrane is joined to the lung, the other to the chest cavity, and between them is a layer of fluid. This allows the outer layers to slide against each other, so the lung can easily inflate and deflate.

LOOK CLOSER
THE PLEURA

pleura

pleura

ribcage

lungs

diaphragm

DID YOU KNOW?

Hiccups are your diaphragm's fault.

Hiccups happen when your diaphragm suddenly tightens. This causes you to unexpectedly pull a lot of air into your lungs. Your body immediately wonders what's going on, and closes the gap in your vocal cords in case there's a problem. That's what makes the 'hiccup' noise. In fact, hiccups are one of the few noises you can make when breathing in.

No one knows why hiccups happen, but lots of people think they know how to cure hiccups. Some crazy cures include:

✳ Swallowing a mouthful of water with your fingers in your ears.

✳ Lying down for several minutes, then standing up really quickly.

✳ Swallowing a mouthful of water while tilting your head back and pulling down on your earlobes.

These 'cures' probably won't work – but they will give anyone watching a good laugh.

HIC!

STRANGE BUT TRUE!

Charles Osborne of Iowa, USA, is said to be the record holder for hiccupping. He hiccupped non-stop for 68 years!

RELAX, AND BREATHE OUT

How long can you hold your breath for? Most people can manage about 20 seconds. After that, your brain stem insists on getting rid of the excess carbon dioxide that has built up, and makes it impossible to hold your breath any longer. But how do you breathe out?

Diaphragm in command

Like breathing in, breathing out is controlled mainly by your diaphragm. The difference is that when you breathe out, your body doesn't have to do any work. The muscles in your diaphragm, ribcage, neck and shoulders just relax. Everything goes back to its non-inflated position, and your lungs deflate, or get smaller. The air in the alveoli is pushed back out – through the bronchioles, then the bronchi, trachea, and finally your mouth or nose.

LOOK CLOSER
BREATHING OUT

Air is forced out through the trachea.

The lungs deflate.

The diaphragm relaxes and moves upwards.

18

Breath temperature

By the time air has circulated through your lungs and been breathed out, it has been warmed (or cooled) by your body. You can easily check this for yourself. On a specially cold or hot day, hold your hand in front of your mouth and blow out. Can you feel a difference in temperature between your breath and the surrounding air?

Kenny G set a world record for the longest note in 1997 by holding E flat on a saxophone for nearly an hour.

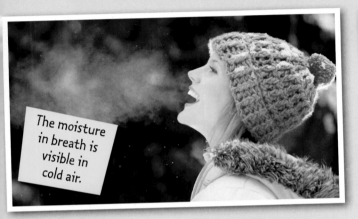

The moisture in breath is visible in cold air.

Moisture in your breath

Your lungs have a moist atmosphere. As air circulates through them, it collects some of the moisture. In fact, the air picks up so much that adults lose about half a litre of water from their body EVERY DAY – just by breathing out!

STRANGE BUT TRUE!
apparently

In Tibet, monks trying to keep warm in the cold winters have developed something called g-tummo. They use special breathing and thinking techniques to raise their body temperatures by up to 1°C. Scientists are still not sure exactly how this works!

See for yourself

Make a fake lung!

1. Cut the base off a plastic bottle.

2. Tie a knot in a balloon, then cut across it at the widest part. Keep the knotted end and throw the other part away.

3. Stretch the wide, cut part of the balloon over the hole at the base of the bottle.

4. Put a straw into the neck of another balloon, and use an elastic band to keep it in place.

5. Push the balloon down through the neck of the bottle and keep the straw sticking out.

6. Seal the opening around the straw with modelling clay. (Make sure you haven't crushed the straw: air has to be able to get into the balloon.)

The balloon inside the bottle acts as a lung. The balloon stretched across the end of the bottle acts as the diaphragm. Pull down on the knot of the bottom balloon, then let it go back to a non-stretched position. What happens to the other balloon?

THE LUNG PROTECTION SQUAD

If your lungs stop working, you can die within minutes. Because of this, they need to be protected from damage. Your lungs aren't QUITE surrounded by body armour – that would make walking around very heavy work. But they do have a very effective equivalent.

Underneath the lungs

Your lungs are in an area of your body called the thoracic cavity. This area inside your chest contains your heart, lungs and food pipe (oesophagus). Below the thoracic cavity is your abdominal cavity. This contains your stomach, liver, kidneys, intestines and other organs. Separating the two cavities is your diaphragm.

The amazing ribcage

Your ribcage is a set of bones that, together with your backbone and breastbone, surround your lungs. Flexible cartilage at the end of each rib links to a bone at the front of your chest – the sternum. The cartilage lets your ribs expand when you breathe in, and also allows the ribcage to act as a shock absorber, taking the force of dangerous blows. These blows either break ribs or tear the cartilage. This REALLY hurts – but it is much better than damaging your lungs.

LOOK CLOSER
RIBCAGE

ribs

sternum

cartilage

lung

Your diaphragm stretches across the bottom of your ribcage. There are holes in it, which allow blood vessels, the oesophagus and nerves to pass through. Muscles connect your diaphragm to the walls of the thoracic cavity and to your spine.

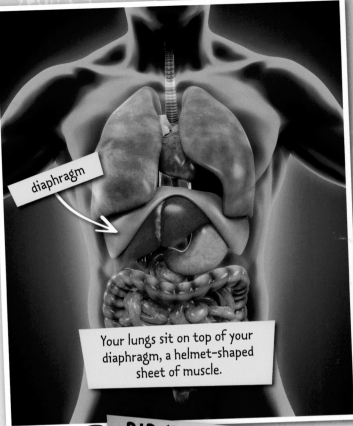

diaphragm

Your lungs sit on top of your diaphragm, a helmet-shaped sheet of muscle.

DON'T TRY THIS AT HOME!

In Victorian times, people who wanted a slimmer waist sometimes wore a device called a corset. It laced up like the top part of a boot, and when the laces were pulled tight, they squeezed the waist. This pushed the lower ribs, diaphragm and some digestive parts inward.

Even girls as young as 10 or 11 wore corsets. The idea was to 'train' their waist to be thinner. The tight corsets prevented their bodies from growing naturally. Some women are even said to have ended up relying on them so much that they found it difficult to sit up without one.

DID YOU KNOW?

Elephants can go snorkelling!

Compared to most other animals, elephants have an extra layer of lung protection. Their lungs are surrounded by tough tissue that joins their lungs to their chest cavity. This strong structure prevents the lungs from being squashed by the pressure of deep water. Without it, an elephant's lungs could collapse if it swam underwater!

Corsets were popular back when no one knew what they did to your insides!

An elephant goes snorkelling.

WHAT'S IN A SNEEZE?

BRILLIANT BODY FACT

Spray from a sneeze can travel over a metre!

Normally, breathing out is just a question of relaxing. Not always, though! Sometimes, air leaves your lungs at high-speed. When something causes your diaphragm to contract suddenly and powerfully, the muscles in your ribs do the same – and you sneeze.

What causes sneezes?

Sneezing has two main causes:

Expelling a foreign body
Sometimes, you breathe in an object that really doesn't belong up your nose. It might be pollen from a plant, dust, pepper or just about anything else that you might breathe in. To expel the foreign body, your brain triggers a sneeze. This is why sneezes usually come in groups: your brain knows that one sneeze isn't usually enough to expel the intruder.

DID YOU KNOW?

Plucking your eyebrows can make you sneeze.

Plucking your eyebrows sometimes triggers a nerve that makes your brain think there's something up your nose. Your brain triggers a sneeze in an attempt to clear the obstruction — which was never there anyway!

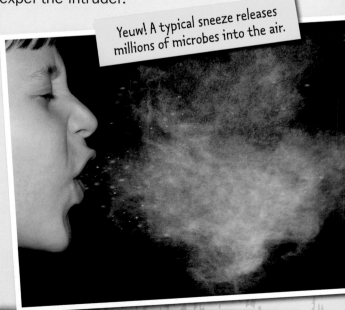

Yeuw! A typical sneeze releases millions of microbes into the air.

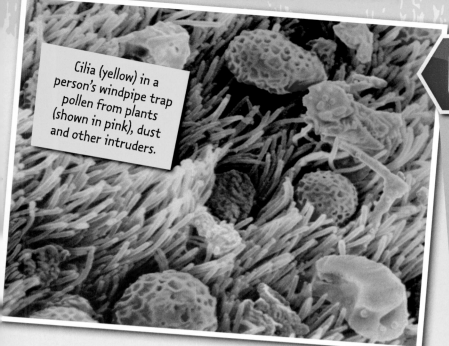

Cilia (yellow) in a person's windpipe trap pollen from plants (shown in pink), dust and other intruders.

DON'T TRY THIS ON A RAINY DAY!

In 2010, a new species of monkey was discovered in the mountains of northern Myanmar. The monkeys have unusual nostrils, which point upwards.

When questioned, local people said they had known about the monkeys forever. They are hard to miss — especially on rainy days. Then, the monkeys are constantly sneezing because of water running into their upturned noses. Some even sit with their heads between their legs, in an attempt to stay dry!

Light

When some people move from dark into light, they sneeze. This is called a photic sneeze. Experts think it is caused by a mix-up between two nerves:

✳ The trigeminal nerve, which sends signals for a sneeze if a foreign body enters your nose.

✳ The optic nerve, which sends messages about light conditions.

These two nerves are very close together, and it seems likely that the signals they carry sometimes get mixed up.

How fast is a sneeze?

Lots of people (especially on the internet) claim that sneezes travel at 100kph, or even 160kph. There's no evidence that people actually do sneeze this fast. Recent studies have recorded people sneezing at 10–39kph. Even so, sneezing is a violent action. People sometimes damage muscles while doing a particularly violent sneeze – especially if they try to stop themselves doing it.

Moving into bright light will cause your optic nerve to react quickly.

STRANGE BUT TRUE!

It's almost unheard of for people to sneeze in their sleep, and practically no one can sneeze with their eyes open. It is almost impossible to stop yourself sneezing, once a sneeze has begun.

WITHOUT LUNGS, YOU CAN'T TALK

Your lungs do more than just power your respiratory system (as if that's not enough!). They also make it possible for you to talk. In fact, they make it possible for you not only to talk. You also need lungs for singing, whistling, whispering and shouting.

larynx, or voice box

How is speech made?

Speech comes from the larynx, which is also called the voice box. It's not actually a box at all. It's a complicated structure of cartilage and muscle. The larynx is at the top of the trachea, the tube leading from your throat down to your lungs.

Stretched across your larynx are two pieces of membrane. These are called the vocal cords. As air flows out of your lungs it passes between the vocal cords. While you are silent, the vocal cords are relaxed and open. When you want to speak, muscles around the larynx pull the cords tight and control the flow of air. The vocal cords vibrate as the air flows past, and this produces sounds.

The sounds your vocal cords produce are made clearer by your mouth, especially your tongue. To prove this to yourself, try speaking with your tongue pressed against the bottom of your mouth the whole time…

LOOK CLOSER
VOCAL CORDS

Usually, the vocal cords are relaxed and open.

The vocal cords pull tight and vibrate when you want to make sound.

STRANGE BUT TRUE!

No school student will be surprised to hear that the world's loudest voice belongs to a teacher! Annalisa Flanagan, from Northern Ireland, was recorded shouting at 121.7 decibels — which is louder than a low-flying jet plane. Her twin sister is almost as loud, at 119 decibels!

DID YOU KNOW?

The vocal cords vibrate a LOT.

For example, to sing the note A above middle C they have to vibrate 440 times per second!

See for yourself

The loudness of your voice depends on how much air is being expelled from your lungs. So does the length of time you can make the noise.

LOUDER	= more air needed.
LONGER	= more air needed.

To test this, try taking a deep breath before quietly saying the names of all the kids in your class. Then take another deep breath and try SHOUTING the names. Do you get as far?

LUNG TROUBLE

For normal, daily life, your lungs have far more capacity than you need. That's why even people with only ONE lung can still do most everyday activities (though they do get out of breath more quickly). Your respiratory system is not indestructible, though, and it can sometimes develop problems.

Asthma

Asthma is a medical condition that makes it hard to get enough air into your lungs. An asthma attack happens when your body reacts to a 'trigger' by narrowing your airways. This makes it harder for air to reach your lungs. Common triggers include house dust, pollen, cigarette smoke, animal fur and exercise.

Asthma cannot be cured, but knowing what is likely to trigger an attack makes it possible to control. If an attack does happen, medicines can help. Many sufferers carry an inhaler, containing medicines that will open their airways.

LOOK CLOSER

ASTHMA

air trapped in alveoli

relaxed smooth muscles

tightened smooth muscles

wall inflamed and thickened

NORMAL AIRWAY

ASTHMATIC AIRWAY

ASTHMATIC AIRWAY DURING ATTACK

Pollution

Pollution is harmful material contained in the air, such as cigarette smoke or gases from vehicle exhausts. Your lungs can cope with a small amount of pollution. The cilia that line your airways move tiny particles of pollution out of the respiratory system. Too much pollution coats the cilia so much that they cannot expel it, and your lungs become clogged up.

Snot – fighting infection

If you've ever had runny nose, you are familiar with one of the main ways your respiratory system defends itself against illness! The mucus, or snot, pouring out of your nose is part of your body's attempt to fight off a virus or bacteria. Viruses and bacteria can affect your airways. As the body tries to fight them off, it produces more mucus, which makes it harder to breathe or even stops your lungs working properly.

A normal lung (left) and a lung damaged by smoking (right). Smoking allows harmful chemicals into your lungs, causing damage.

DID YOU KNOW?

The common cold really IS common.

More people catch the common cold every year than any other sickness of the respiratory system. It is the cause of the largest number of visits to the doctor, and the most missed days from school and work. Some experts think the common cold may be the commonest illness of ALL.

In many cities, some people wear face masks. They aim to keep out pollution and germs.

DON'T TRY THIS AT HOME!

Well, you could TRY these 'cures' next time you have a cold. There's just no evidence that they would work.

Wrap your throat in dirty socks (England)
Make sure you grease the outside of your throat with chicken fat or lard, or the cure won't work. (Hint: it won't work anyway.)

Make yourself some lizard soup (Hong Kong, China)
Actually, this soup is not made using only dried lizards. It also contains yams and Chinese dates.

STRANGE BUT TRUE!

The bronchi in your lungs have taste buds, a bit like the ones in your mouth. Researchers have found that bitter tastes cause the lungs to relax. This knowledge may one day be used to treat asthma.

MAINTENANCE AND SERVICING

Everything you do depends on your body getting oxygen. If your lungs do not work properly, you may not always get enough oxygen.
Things that you think about – like maths tests – and those that you don't – like growing fingernails – would all become much harder.
So, how can you keep your lungs in tip-top shape?

① Don't smoke, or be around smoke

Cigarette smoke, whether it comes from a cigarette you are smoking or someone else's, is very harmful to your lungs and respiratory system. Find out more on page 27.

② Campaign for clean air

Air pollution has similar harmful effects to smoking. Encourage politicians and other leaders to fight for clean air and you will help everyone's lungs, not only your own.

BRILLIANT BODY FACT

Playing a wind instrument helps your lungs to work better!

③ Run around!

Exercising regularly is probably the best thing you can do for your lungs. Exercise makes your lungs breathe harder. The muscles you use to breathe get stronger and more flexible. Your lungs get better at exchanging carbon dioxide for oxygen. You also increase the amount of air your lungs can take in with a single breath.

As well as all these benefits, exercise makes your body better at using the oxygen your lungs provide. Your heart gets stronger and able to pump faster. Your blood vessels deliver the oxygen better. Exercise may even

Exercise is good for your lungs.

make you smarter: experts have shown that kids who start exercising soon also get better marks at school.

④ Avoid indoor pollution

Avoid indoor air pollution. This can come from wood and coal fires, pet dander, or even mould on walls or food. Keeping the indoors clean and well ventilated will reduce the risks.

⑤ Eat lung-loving foods

Surprisingly, research has shown that some foods are good for your lungs. In particular, people who eat plenty of broccoli, cauliflower, cabbage, pak choi, kale and similar vegetables are less likely to get lung cancer.

Pet hair and dander can irritate some people's airways.

STRANGE BUT TRUE!

Playing a wind instrument can help asthma sufferers control their condition by making their lungs stronger. In fact, in Australia some asthma sufferers have been taught to play the didgeridoo, as part of their treatment!

A balanced diet includes plenty of fruit and vegetables.

The most famous lung dish is Scottish haggis. Traditionally, this is made from the heart and lungs of a lamb, mixed with other ingredients, and tied up inside a sheep's stomach before being cooked. It tastes better than it sounds or looks!

DID YOU KNOW?

Lung is a popular meal.

Not human lung, obviously! But many of the animals we eat have lungs, and around the world they are a popular food. In Greece, lamb lungs are used to make soup for Easter; in Asia, they are cut into strips and fried. In the USA, though, you can't eat lungs — it's illegal.

BREATHTAKING WORDS!

abdominal cavity an area of your body between your chest and hips, which contains your stomach, liver, kidneys, intestines and other organs

airways the multiple passages that allow air to travel to and from your lungs

blood vessels the tubes carrying blood around your body

capillaries the smallest type of blood vessels, with walls so thin that gases and some chemicals can pass through

carbon dioxide a gas that in excess is poisonous to humans. Its chemical formula is CO_2.

cartilage the tough tissue that connects parts of the human body, in particular bones

didgeridoo a hollow wooden tube used as a musical instrument, originally by Aboriginal Australians

epiglottis a leaf-shaped flap of skin in your throat, which changes its position depending on whether you are breathing or swallowing

freediver a person who swims in deep water, without using scuba-diving equipment that would allow them to breathe below the surface

inhaler a device carried by people who have asthma. The inhaler contains chemicals that are breathed into the lungs and help the person to breathe normally.

instinct an action that is done from birth and happens automatically

lungs the two air-filled organs in your chest, where oxygen is removed from air and passed into your blood, and CO_2 is removed from your blood and breathed out

membrane very thin tissue

microbe a microorganism that exists as just one cell, and can only be seen with a microscope

mucus a slimy substance produced by the body that traps dirt and microbes. It also lubricates some parts of the body.

nasal passages the airways that connect your nostrils to your throat

oesophagus the pipe that you swallow food down. It leads from the throat to the stomach.

organ part of your body that has a special function. Some important organs include the heart, brain, lungs and liver.

oxygen a colourless gas that is present in the air. Humans breathe in air and use the oxygen to release energy from food.

pet dander old skin that has flaked off and then been trapped in the fur of a pet animal

pollen tiny, powdery grains that are released by plants

thoracic cavity the area inside your chest, protected by your ribs, which contains your heart, lungs and oesophagus

vocal cords the structures at the top of your trachea, which change shape when air moves across them, allowing you to make different sounds

BREATHLESS INFORMATION

Are you gasping for more information? Here are some good places to find out more about the lungs and respiratory system:

BOOKS TO READ

Go Figure: *A Maths Journey Through the Human Body*, Anne Rooney, Wayland 2014

How to build a Human Body, Tom Jackson, Scholastic 2013

Mind Webs: *Human Body*, Anna Claybourne, Wayland 2014

The World in Infographics: *The Human Body*, Jon Richards and Ed Simkins, Wayland 2013

Truth or Busted: *The Fact or Fiction Behind Human Bodies*, Paul Mason, Wayland 2014

WEBSITES

http://kidshealth.org/kid/htbw/lungs.html

This website is a really good place to find out all sorts of information about the human body. It has an excellent section on the respiratory system.

http://www.childrensuniversity.manchester. ac.uk/interactives/science/exercise/

The Children's University of Manchester, UK, has all sorts of information for kids, presented in the form of labelled illustrations. It includes a section explaining the main benefits of exercise.

PLACES TO VISIT

In London, the **Science Museum** has regular exhibitions and displays explaining how the body works. The museum is at:

Exhibition Road
South Kensington
London SW7 2DD

The Science Museum also has a good website:
www.sciencemuseum.org.uk/whoami/findoutmore

The **Natural History Museum** has an amazing 'Human Biology Gallery' where you can find out all about the amazing human body, from how your brain and other organs work together, to the many jobs your blood does. The museum is at:

The Natural History Museum
Cromwell Road
London, SW7 5BD

The museum also has a good website:
http://www.nhm.ac.uk/visit-us/galleries/blue-zone/human-biology/

INDEX

WAYLAND

Published in paperback
in 2016 by Wayland
Copyright © Wayland, 2016
All rights reserved.

Editor: Annabel Stones
Designer: Rocket Design (East Anglia) Ltd
Consultant: John Clancy, Former Senior
Lecturer in Applied Human Physiology
Proofreader: Susie Brooks

Dewey Number: 612.1-dc23
ISBN: 978 0 7502 9740 0
Library ebook ISBN: 978 0 7502 9389 1
10 9 8 7 6 5 4 3 2 1

Wayland, an imprint of
Hachette Children's Group
Part of Hodder & Stoughton
Carmelite House
50 Victoria Embankment
London EC4Y 0DZ

An Hachette UK Company
www.hachette.co.uk
www.hachettechildrens.co.uk
Printed in China

Artwork: Ian Thompson: p5 r, p8;
Stefan Chabluk: p3 t, p7 c, p9 br,
p11 t, p13 t, p19 br.

Picture credits: Getty Images: p4 Barcroft Media
/ contributor, p9 bl Mike Powell / staff, p13 b
Samo Vidic / contributor, p22 William Radcliffe,
p25 r Chiaki Nozu / contributor; iStockphoto:
p19 cl FangXiaNuo; Mary Evans: p21 cl Mary
Evans Picture Library; Science Photo Library: 9 tl
ALFRED PASIEKA, p10 D. PHILLIPS, p23 tl EDDY
GRAY; Shutterstock: Cover, p3 cr, p3 b, p5 bl, p6,
p7 br, p12, p14 bl, p14 br, p15 bl, p15 br, p16,
p17 tr, p17 br, p18, p19 tr Joe Seer, p20, p21
tr, p21br, p23 bl, p24, p25 t, p26, p27 tr, p27 br
TonyV3112, p28 l, p28 br, p29 t, p29 c, p29 bc.
CC Wikimedia Commons: p11 b.

MIX
Paper from
responsible sources
FSC
www.fsc.org FSC® C104740